Easy to Play Violin Airs and Ballads

Gene Clarke

WWW.MELBAY.COM

Foreword

Many beautiful melodies – both folk songs and "composed" popular songs – originated in Great Britain and the United States during the nineteenth and early twentieth centuries. *Easy to Play Violin Airs and Ballads* is a collection of twenty-five of these tunes arranged in a way that can be enjoyed by student and amateur violinists of all ages.

All of the tunes are written entirely in first position, with bowing indications and fingerings for any unusual accidentals marked. Chord names are included for accompaniment by a guitarist or player of any chord-capable instrument. Every song can also be played along with the corresponding title in *Easy to Play Viola Airs and Ballads* and *Easy to Play Cello Airs and Ballads.*

I thank Mr. William Bay for encouraging me to write this book and helping me find the tunes herein. I hope all of you enjoy playing these melodies as much as I have enjoyed collecting, arranging and playing through them!

Gene Clarke

Contents

Title	Page
All the Pretty Horses	4
Barbara Allen	5
Bonnie Dundee	6
Botany Bay	7
In the Days of Forty-Nine	8
George Collins	9
Handsome Molly	10
I Am a Pilgrim	11
I Ride an Old Paint	12
In the Good Old Summertime	13
Listen to the Mockingbird	14
The Little Old Log Cabin in the Woods	15
Lynchburg Town	16
The Old Oaken Bucket	17
Only a Bird in a Gilded Cage	18
Over the Garden Wall	19
Pretty Saro	20
Sweet Polly Oliver	21
The Banks of the Ohio	22
The Letter Edged in Black	23
The Mermaid's Song	24
The Mist-Covered Mountains	25
The Parting Glass	26
The Rose of Tralee	27
The Wagoner's Lad	28

All the Pretty Horses

Fingerpicking or Strumming

Traditional Lullaby
arranged by Gene Clarke

Barbara Allen

Traditional Scottish Ballad
arranged by Gene Clarke

Slowly and sadly

Bonnie Dundee

Scottish Folk Tune
arranged by Gene Clarke

Botany Bay

Australian Folk Song
arranged by Gene Clarke

In the Days Of Forty-Nine

Traditional American Ballad
arranged by Gene Clarke

Steadily-not too fast

George Collins

Old English Ballad
arranged by Gene Clarke

Slowly

Handsome Molly

Traditional Old-Time Song
arranged by Gene Clarke

I Am a Pilgrim

Southern Gospel Tune, 1864
arranged by Gene Clarke

I Ride an Old Paint

Cowboy Song, Early 1900's
arranged by Gene Clarke

Loping along

In the Good Old Summertime

Ren Shields and George Evans, 1902
arranged by Gene Clarke

Listen to the Mockingbird

Septimus Winner, 1855
arranged by Gene Clarke

The Little Old Log Cabin in the Woods

William S. Hays, 1871
arranged by Gene Clarke

Wistfully

fingerpicking or strumming

Lynchburg Town

Frank Spencer, 1848
arranged by Gene Clarke

The Old Oaken Bucket

George F. Kiallmark, 1826
arranged by Gene Clarke

Nostalgically

Only a Bird in a Gilded Cage

Arthur J. Lamb and Harry von Tilzer, 1900
arranged by Gene Clarke

Moderate waltz

Over the Garden Wall

Harry Hunter and George D. Fox, 1879
arranged by Gene Clarke

Pretty Saro

Traditional American Tune, Early 1900's
arranged by Gene Clarke

Lively

Sweet Polly Oliver

English Broadside Ballad, 1840
arranged by Gene Clarke

Gracefully

The Banks of the Ohio

19th Century Ballad
arranged by Gene Clarke

The Letter Edged in Black

Hattie Nevada, 1899
arranged by Gene Clarke

Sorrowfully

The Mermaid's Song

Scottish Air
arranged by Gene Clarke

Moderately Slow

The Mist-Covered Mountains

Traditional Scottish Air
arranged by Gene Clarke

Slowly

The Parting Glass

Traditional Irish Tune
arranged by Gene Clarke

Solemnly

The Rose of Tralee

19th Century Irish Folk Song
arranged by Gene Clarke

Slow and sentimental

The Wagoner's Lad

Old Time Ballad, 1907
arranged by Gene Clarke

Moving along